A Year
Goes Round

A Year Goes Round

Poems for the Months

November · December · January · February · March · April · May · June · July · August · September · October

Karen B. Winnick

Wordsong · Boyds Mills Press

Copyright © 2001 by Karen B. Winnick

Published by Wordsong
Boyds Mills Press, Inc.
A Highlights Company
815 Church Street
Honesdale, Pennsylvania 18431
Printed in China

U.S. Cataloging-in-Publication Data
(Library of Congress Standards)

Winnick, Karen B.
A year goes round : poems for the months / Karen B. Winnick. — 1st ed.
[32] p. : col. ill. ; cm.
Summary: Poems and paintings depict the events
and activities during each month of the year.
ISBN 1-56397-898-9
1. Months—Poetry. 2. American poetry. I. Title.
811/. 54 21 2001 CIP   AC
99-69931

First edition, 2001
Book designed by Karen Winnick and Jason Thorne
The text of this book is set in 14-point Hiroshige.

Visit our Web site at www.boydsmillspress.com

10 9 8 7 6 5 4 3 2 1

For my family,
and in loving memory of Myra Cohn Livingston

CONTENTS

WHITE

Outside my window
the glare is bright.

Fresh snow changed
the world last night.

Streets and rooftops
glisten white.

WINTER BEACH

Waves swoosh and rise,
rumble and roar
to foamy peaks
Waves swell and soar.

Tumbling, crashing
down, down they pound
Over the rocks
with a breathless sound.

SNOW ANGEL

I flop into a snowdrift bed
both my arms and legs outspread,
close my eyes, lie icicle-still,
on the top of a windy hill.
Frozen angel in marble relief—
numb nose, chattering teeth.

WIND

Flags flap to and fro,
Scraps of paper blow.
Gates on fences swing
Wind oh Wind oh Wind . . .

Kites of paper soar.
Rivers swell and roar.
Bells on steeples ring
Wind oh Wind oh Wind . . .

Trunks of trees bend down.
Leaves go swirling 'round.
Blades of grasses sing
Wind oh Wind oh Wind . . .

QUIET MORNING

Early in the morning
dog, book and me
spend quiet moments,
just we three.

Snuggled by the window,
chin on my knee,
close to the raindrops,
dog, book and me.

TRYOUTS

Hey kid,
You're next.
Take your place.

Push that cap
off your face.

Choke the bat.
Keep some space.

Spread your feet.
Tie your lace.

Hey kid,
Most of all,
Don't forget—

Watch the ball!

WET

Dripping down my slicker
Spilling off my bonnet
Flooding through my sneaker
Filling up my pocket

Streaming from my muffler
Seeping down my kneesocks
Soaking through my sweater
All of April's raindrops.

PARADE

Rat-a-tat-tat,
Rat-a-tat-tat,
My heels start to tap
at the beat of the drum.
Rat-a-tat-tat,
Rat-a-tat-tat,
I clap with my hands
and snap with my thumb.
Rat-a-tat-tat,
Rat-a-tat-tat,
I love a parade.
Here I come!

WELCOME BACK

Frog,
I missed you when
the pond froze thick with ice.

You disappeared but then—
you must have checked the clock.

Now you're here with spring,
back sunning on your rock.

MY DOG

I tickle her belly
and scratch her ear.
I pat her head
to say I care.

She pokes my nose
and sniffs my hands.
She licks my cheek.
She understands.

SWINGING

Swinging high
over trees,

shoes are skimming
tips of leaves . . .

Higher up
pushing free . . .

there is just
sky and me.

THE WAVE

It's coming! Run fast!
Get out of its way!
This one's going to last.
Get out of its way!
An ear-splitting blast
and a thunderous spray!
It's coming! Run fast!
Get out of its way!

THE PLAYGROUND

My friend has gone away,
There's nothing much to do.
It's empty here today,
My friend has gone away.
I want him back to play,
I don't want someone new.
My friend has gone away,
There's nothing much to do.

SAND PICTURE

Close to the shore,
I draw in the sand,
a house with chimney,
smoke in the air.

A man at the door,
a road dug by hand,
I step back to see—
They disappear!

CITY SUMMER

Sun sizzles the bricks,
steaming our street.
We sweat and swelter
from summer heat.

The hydrant bursts.
Water spurts out.
It chills our skin.
"Cold rain," we shout.

SUMMER'S END

Good-bye to bare feet,
to August's late heat,

to swims in the sea,
sleepovers for three,

to campfire nights,
long days of light.

In the wink of an eye,
all of summer—gone by.

DODGE BALL

The kids go up
against the wall.
They make a line.
One throws the ball.

They start to scream,
take off and run.
I watch those kids.
They're having fun.

Next time I see
them come this way,
I'm going to ask,
"Can one more play?"

MY SHADOW

My shadow moves along the wall.
    A jump, a hop and one swift skip.
My shadow's long and lean and tall,
    the way he moves along the wall.
A leg goes out, my shadow falls.
    A jump, a hop and one bad trip.
My shadow moves along the wall.
    A jump, a hop and one swift skip.

DISGUISES

Just for tonight,
for Halloween,
we'll put on masks.
We won't be seen.

If someone asks,
"Now, who are they?"
please promise me
that you won't say!

FALL LEAVES

I'll toss the leaves,
fling them high

up like feathers
to fill the sky.

Or gather piles
along the ground

to be my cushions
when I fall down.

FEEDING THE GOOSE

Goose, Goose,
come over here.
I've tossed you crumbs.
See, everywhere.

Goose, Goose,
please come and eat
out of my hand.
Close, so we meet.

FIRST SNOW

Everywhere I go,
Snow
Snow
Snow.
Stuck to my boots,
Crumbled in my hand,
What shall I do
with cold white sand?

ON STAGE

Hums and whispers
everywhere,
my stomach gurgles.
    "Shhh, down there!"

Both my cheeks
begin to burn.
The music starts
    and now . . . *my turn!*

COLD OUTSIDE

Toggle coat.
Muffler at my throat.
Fur in each boot.
Heavy snowsuit.

Wooly headband.
Mitten on each hand.
Hood on my hair.
Long underwear.

It's warm inside here.